Remembering Who I am

MABEL CAMPBELL

BALBOA.PRESS
A DIVISION OF HAY HOUSE

Copyright © 2020 Mabel Campbell.

All rights reserved. No part of this book may be used or reproduced by any means, graphic, electronic, or mechanical, including photocopying, recording, taping or by any information storage retrieval system without the written permission of the author except in the case of brief quotations embodied in critical articles and reviews.

Balboa Press books may be ordered through booksellers or by contacting:

Balboa Press
A Division of Hay House
1663 Liberty Drive
Bloomington, IN 47403
www.balboapress.co.uk
UK TFN: 0800 0148647 (Toll Free inside the UK)
UK Local: 02036 956325 (+44 20 3695 6325 from outside the UK)

Because of the dynamic nature of the Internet, any web addresses or links contained in this book may have changed since publication and may no longer be valid. The views expressed in this work are solely those of the author and do not necessarily reflect the views of the publisher, and the publisher hereby disclaims any responsibility for them.

The author of this book does not dispense medical advice or prescribe the use of any technique as a form of treatment for physical, emotional, or medical problems without the advice of a physician, either directly or indirectly. The intent of the author is only to offer information of a general nature to help you in your quest for emotional and spiritual well-being. In the event you use any of the information in this book for yourself, which is your constitutional right, the author and the publisher assume no responsibility for your actions.

Any people depicted in stock imagery provided by Getty Images are models, and such images are being used for illustrative purposes only. Certain stock imagery © Getty Images.

Print information available on the last page.

ISBN: 978-1-9822-8205-9 (sc)
ISBN: 978-1-9822-8204-2 (e)

Balboa Press rev. date: 09/21/2020

Contents

Acknowledgements ix
Introduction xi

| Chapter 1 | Self-Awareness .... 1 |

Chapter 2	Ways of Connecting to Source 11
	Meditation 12
	Walking in Nature 13
	Journaling 15
	Yoga 16
	Reflexology 17
	Dance 17
	Vision Boards 17
	Foraging 20

Chapter 3	Self-Care 21
	Physical Self-Care 22
	Decluttering 23
	Emotional Self-Care 27
	Social Self-Care 27
	Spiritual Self-Care 29
	The Serenity Prayer 29
	Church 30

Chapter 4	Letting Go	32
	Dealing with Childhood Trauma	35
	Forgiveness	37
	Letting Go of the Future	38
	Letting Go of the Need to Prove Yourself	39
	Letting Go of Relationships	39
	Letting Go of Fear	40
	Getting Help	41
Chapter 5	Spiritual Surrender	46
	Pray	47
	Let Go	48
	Listen	49
Chapter 6	The Essence of Who You Are	51
	Learning	51
	Joy	53
	Trust	54
	Your Spiritual Core	57
	Looking Ahead	59
Chapter 7	Spiritual Disciplines	61
	Establishing Good Habits	61
	Have a Reason Why You Should Do It	62
	Remove Obstacles and Excuses	62
	Have a Trigger	62
	Reduce Your Expectations	63
	An Example	63
	Taking Time in Solitude	64
	The Big Thing	66

Chapter 8	What Is Love?.. 68
	Beliefs... 69
	Religion and Self-Help............................. 70
	Sense of Self 71
Chapter 9	Creating a Life That You Love.................. 73
	Freedom 74
	Connecting with Helpers............................ 77
	Spring Seeds 80
	Investment in you for others 81
	Social Farming and its benefits 82
	The Future 84

Charts and Diagrams.. 85
The Chakras 85
The Wheel of Life... 89
A Sample Self-Care Plan 90

Acknowledgements

I would like to thank the many people who have supported me throughout my healing journey to now and who have encouraged me to write and publish this book.

To Angela Burke my therapist and healer I owe the deepest of gratitude. Many times, over the course of 20 plus years she has challenged me to my core, releasing painful memories and emotions throughout. Shedding light on the dark within as I journeyed.

To Eamon Baker who inspired me to write my first piece of writing which was included in the "Softly Spoken" book based on the loss of my brother from the conflict in Northern Ireland.

To Jenny for her help in shaping content for this book and Balboa Press the publisher for their help and assistance, designing and printing.

To all the other therapists, yoga practitioners, and life coaches who have inspired me to learn, grow and evolve from my studies. You know who you are.

To my family and friends, for being there and supporting me, for their patience and understanding. Some of you will get this writing and some will not. We need to have compassion for those who are not yet ready to live in the light but hopefully one day will.

Now is a time of great change for all. It's time to slow down, to reflect, to go within, to be seen, heard and allowed to speak our truth, to not judge, to breathe, to spend time in nature, to be healed, to love and be loved, finding peace and happiness.

Introduction

It's almost impossible to not parent ourselves similarly to the way we were parented as kids. If our caretakers dealt with us in a hurtful manner, then as adults we will find all kinds of ways to pass on that unsolved pain to ourselves and others. If we were frequently ignored, blamed, chastised, or abused physically or emotionally, then we will continue to beat ourselves up. We follow the patterns that we have been taught. This is what happened to me in the way I was brought up—or my conditioning, as it is called.

My parents had a tough life, and so did their parents. I was brought up on a rural mountain sheep farm in the 1960s, the youngest of eleven. My dad died when I was four, and my mother was left with a handful. Mum carried on the farm, and my older siblings helped her. She did the best she could within her capabilities. Some of us went out to work, and some of us were sent to live with aunts and uncles. As the youngest, I stayed at home and helped her as much as I could. My mum held on to the farm until my eldest brother was able to take it over. Then he got married, and my mum and I moved out to a cottage. My childhood was a struggle. Starved of love, I felt very much alone. In the early eighties, when I was going on eighteen, I got pregnant out of wedlock. At that time, I was told that I had brought a huge amount of shame to my family. They simply didn't know how to handle me, so I had to leave home.

I wanted to keep the child, my daughter. I went to live with my soon-to-be husband's parents, and my mother told my brothers and sisters to stay away from me. My mother-in-law was grand and supported me the best she could. I got married, but it still was very tough. I went on to have two other kids. It was stressful, but I thought I had to toughen up; it was the way things were.

I worked for a time as a sales representative for an insurance company, in a male-dominated environment. It seemed that I was living my life with a mask on. It felt like everyone else was wearing a mask too—that none of us was real. I felt I needed the mask to cope with life and other people.

It was a good job, paid well, and provided for my family. My children were doing well at school. They were all I had, and every minute, I strived to carry on, to support them. Success meant having it all, but there was an emptiness deep down. I was searching for something. At the time, I never really understood what I was searching for. On the outside, I suppose they would have seen me as successful, but bubbling underneath, that certainly wasn't how I felt. I had another child in 1992, I carried on, and I didn't question my life. I continued to work while my husband looked after the child until I was paid off, being labelled as clinically depressed.

I spent three years in counselling. The counselling was grand, but it was merely a talking therapy. We talked the life out of what was going on, but it never really did get in touch with the deep-seated stuff—my feelings or emotions.

I became the label with which I was diagnosed. I became more depressed, and it took me down a dark hole. I was forced to look at myself, my family, and my background.

I wouldn't take antidepressants. Some would say I was stubborn, but my upbringing had taught me not to be seen as a failure, and to struggle. I had a fighting spirit just like my mother. Like attracts like; when I struggled, I inflicted more pain on myself, and the pattern continued—a vicious cycle.

I picked myself up and went back to college. I completed an IT and Professional Development for Women certificate, and I went on to complete an HND in care practice. I gained experience in working with different client groups.

I got a job working with people who suffered as a result of the violent conflict in Northern Ireland. It was grand at the start, but listening and supporting people who had either suffered trauma or were trying to cope with PTSD was difficult, and my own trauma started to surface.

This led me to explore the world of healing. I was drawn to reiki, and I studied self-awareness. I began to wake up and seek to better understand my life and why I was the way I was.

The cycle of dysfunction and abuse had left me blaming myself, but it seemed to me that I had grown up fragmented, with no real sense of self at all. As I studied, the process of taking the layers off the onion began.

I continued to do a diploma in healing, learning all about chakras. Within a group setting, I was immersed to shift my suppressed emotions using the five rhythms of dance devised by Gabrielle Roth. I danced and was challenged to my very core by a reiki facilitator. There was a lot of mirror work completed. First there was fear, and behind the fear came the anger, and behind the anger came a flood of sadness, and then there was joy and compassion.

Rhythm	Emotion	Stage of Life	Way of Perceiving	Aspect of Self
Flowing	Fear	Birth	Being	Body
Staccato	Anger	Childhood	Loving	Heart
Chaos	Sadness	Puberty	Knowing	Mind
Lyrical	Joy	Maturity	Seeing	Soul
Stillness	Compassion	Death	Healing	Spirit

This created a massive shift in my life. I started to connect and understand my behaviours and where my anger was coming from. I was projecting the anger onto myself and my family when it should have been aimed at those who inflicted it on me. I started to look at the relationship I had with my mother, my father, and the siblings I grew up with, as well as their impact on my life. I started to connect with my coping strategies, my addictions. I learned why I was using food for protection and why I was stuffing down my feelings.

Whenever I started in healing, I didn't realize all the possible connections. A lot of people who need healing are put off by talk of reiki and chakras and what they might regard as New Age nonsense. But once you peel all that away, it comes down to this: it is love that heals, rather than any of the techniques. We simply use the techniques to help us to get to know, accept, and love ourselves.

> *It is love that heals, rather than any of the techniques. We use the techniques to help us to get to know, accept and love ourselves.*
>
> —Doriel Hall, *Healing with Meditation*

Whenever I have been in the depths of depression and going through hard times, I haven't recognised how powerful it can be. You can heal your life. You can go to any healer, but they are used as a channel, really, for the love to come through from the Spirit of God, or the Higher Power, or however you choose to see it, if you are willing. It's all down to you. It's not belief in the power of the healer; it's belief in the healing and belief in yourself—that you can heal.

I read many self-help books, seeking more awareness and understanding to include my social programming. I got into meditation and walking. I stayed on in my spiritual path—most of the time.

When the going was good, I thought I could survive without the commitment to my spiritual practices, but I have always had to come back to it. I learned that when something in my life wasn't right, it wasn't, so I worked on it and took another layer off the onion. The process of letting go kept going.

If there is any lesson from this book, it is to seek help

and keep reaching out until you find the healer who helps you heal your life. Listen to the quiet voice deep within. When someone is pushing your buttons, it's a sign to look within again. I did, and you can do it too.

CHAPTER 1

Self-Awareness

Self-awareness is the first step in creating what you want and mastering your life. Where you focus your attention, your emotions, reactions, personality, and behaviour will determine where you go in life.

Having self-awareness allows you to see where your thoughts and emotions are taking you. It also allows you to take control of your emotions, behaviour, and personality so you can make the changes you want. Until you are aware in the moment of your thoughts, emotions, words, and behaviour, you will have difficulty making changes in the direction of your life.

Self-awareness includes awareness of the body, awareness of the mind, awareness of your emotions, awareness of your relationships, and awareness of your environment. Pay attention to all of these.

As Anthony de Mello, a spiritual teacher and writer, says, "Come home to yourself." Slow down and observe yourself. This book offers you the chance to slow down.

> *Self-reflection helps you to understand. You can only change what you understand. You repress what you do not understand and what you are not aware of.*
>
> *When you understand it, it will change.*
>
> —Anthony de Mello

As you work on yourself and take notice of what's going on through the process of self-reflection, it will lead you on your journey of personal growth, positivity, and happiness.

I had a lot of not-so-nice experiences in childhood, but with growth and personal development, I am able to use them in a positive way. My journey has led me to ask questions. What do I want out of life? Who am I, and what do I want to do and leave as a legacy for my children and grandchildren?

The writer Eckhart Tolle makes suggestions on the question "What do I want from life?" He suggests you ask yourself a more powerful question, such as "What does life want from me?"

Most of the time we rush around, and we don't have

time to reflect. Now I've gotten to a place where I do, but the getting there has been an ongoing learning experience.

There are many ways to self-awareness. One is meditation and slowing down to get out of the routine. I call it me time. My mum would have worked herself under the table. She was always out in the fields, putting everyone else before herself. I used to do that too, but I don't do it anymore.

That's taught to us by society as well. We get it from the TV, we get it from schooling, we get it from the work ethic that we must work hard to get money, and we have been brainwashed to a certain extent that we have to have the big house or the flashy car—and that if other people have them, then we must have them too.

But then you start to ask, Does it bring happiness? Does all the money in the word bring happiness? Overworking is an addiction. It's a way to escape your feelings. There are people who use gambling or buying stuff to escape their feelings. Smoking, drinking, and even exercise can be an addiction. We can do all these things to avoid pain.

I used to get caught up in people's dramas. I used to listen to gossip. Again, you can learn why are you doing that. If you are talking about your neighbour, that makes you feel good, but think about why you need that. What are you getting out of it? You're always getting something out of it. You may be addicted to chitter-chattering to feed your own self-esteem by putting down other people.

I think it's important to question addictions and discover what you are avoiding. Ask yourself why. What's the pain in your past that you are trying to avoid?

There are certain people that I call your teachers. You constantly get into dramas with them because they have something to teach you. They have a different point of view, so they push your buttons.

The best way to deal with that situation is to meet them where they are at and accept that they have a different point of view. If you don't have that awareness, you let your emotions control you, and you get into the hot stuff. Then it causes an argument. If you listen to your feelings, you realise it is important to understand where they are coming from. It's telling you something. It's there for a reason.

The lower self (the stuff that you do automatically, without thinking) is based on what you have carried with you from childhood. You—yourself as a whole—operate on your understanding of that. Most people operate on their lower-self mentality without questioning it. They go about their day-to-day lives without self-awareness. You are not fully aware of those beliefs, and you take them as part of who you are—until you start to question them.

A lot of our beliefs are formed from our parents and from our schooling, our conditioning and our culture, and our understanding of how society operates. Until you start to question those beliefs, something within you will feel not right.

Of course, you can't question everything all the time. Sometimes if you are in that frame of mind, you can get stuck in overthinking things. When you replace the question 'Why is this happening to me?' with 'What is this trying to teach me?' then everything shifts.

For example, if you are brought up with the belief that life is a struggle, that's what you will make it. That will put stress on you, and you will attract stressful situations. That's the law of attraction: you tend to get what you believe you will get.

What you complain about is what you are focused on, so you need to change your focus, or else the law of attraction will bring you more things to complain about. If you say to someone, 'I don't want to argue,' the universe hears that you want to argue. If you say, 'I can't handle this work,' the universe takes it to mean that you want more work that you can't handle!

When someone pushes my buttons, I'll ask why I have a difficulty with that person. I'll take that to my healer, and she'll work on it. She'll work on the cellular memory and take me right in to the core. Then I release the pain and release the memory, and I don't have any bother with that person again. That person disappears out of my life.

You may not think that things that happened in your childhood have affected you, but that is what happened to me. I suppressed a lot of those early memories, and I know that when I work with my healer, things will come up for me that spark some memory.

That person is always there to push the buttons because you have a lesson to learn. You keep attracting experiences until you realise what it is that you need to learn. Those people are in your life to teach you something. Isn't it amazing?

You realise something is wrong when you become aware of repeating the pattern but don't yet understand why you keep repeating it, and so you are unable to change. I would always have had problems with my weight, and I never understood why I was having those problems. As I started to remove the layers of the onion, I realised I was using the weight to keep people away from me. Because of the early abuse, I had little sense of self-worth. I wasn't totally present within my body because I didn't want to take responsibility for it.

Now, I would say that I deserve better, back but then, I didn't think that I did. That's what self-sabotage is: I was putting myself down. Once you work on where the blame and the shame really lies, then you can start to take back your power and build yourself up again.

I would have been angry at home and never understood it. I was directing that anger at my husband and my children, but that was not where it should have been going at all. If you are brought up starved of love, you search outside yourself all the time, looking for love and not finding it, until you start to love yourself. The love must start with yourself. Until you realise that, you will keep looking outside yourself and blaming other things in your life. You must take responsibility.

Once I went for healing, everything that was there was brought back to me. I had to go within to look at myself and take my part of the responsibility for what I was doing. My problems with my weight were giving me an external excuse for being miserable, and I hadn't the self-awareness to understand why I felt the way I was feeling. It was like an addiction. Within that mindset, food was my comfort.

The anger was another addiction. You can't change these things until you fully understand why or where it comes from. It's hard to admit it, but as you take responsibility, you feel that it's not a power without—it's a power within.

What is addiction, really?

> *It is a sign, a signal, a symptom of distress, it is language that tells us about a plight that must be understood*
>
> —Alice Miller, *Breaking Down the Wall of Silence*

To get to that initial point of awareness, you need to pay attention to your feelings. If you feel that something is wrong, it probably is. Your feelings are not something that is forced upon you, or that you must struggle to suppress. They are there for a reason, to tell you what needs to change inside you.

I think I learned the hard way. If someone had told me at an earlier stage to listen to my feelings, to reflect on why I was feeling the way I was, it would have been easier. I think I ignored my feelings to survive. I had to. But once you start to work on the pain, to release and let go, then you recognise your true feelings, and you don't need to suppress them anymore.

I think the heart has more creativity than the mind. The mind is a strange thing. It wants certainty and control. If you go with your heart, it's more authentic—it's your true self that's coming through.

If you suppress your emotions for a long time, self-analysis is very hard. I didn't let my gut feeling guide me because I wanted to please people, to seek approval from others. Sometimes parents encourage their children in education, or to do things that the parents missed out on doing, but the children really want to play the guitar or do something else. If you don't have a solid grounding or sense of self, it is very easy to do things to please other people. It's a sad way to live a life.

I had no conscious sense of awareness that I was doing that, but deep down, there was a trigger there. I know now I should have listened to myself. The signs were there, but I didn't recognise them. Your feelings always come back and tell you that there is something under the surface, but you carry on until you think to yourself, 'Whose life am I living here? Am I leading my own or someone else's?'

I must admit that I followed my husband and his passions. I was carrying the weight of it; I took on the responsibility. That was what my mother would have done. That was the pattern: to take on responsibility.

A lot of women do that. I think it's to do with oppression, because women were not seen as being equal. I would have put in a lot of work into my relationships, but it wasn't me that got the praise. That's where I think the oppression is. I have started to think a lot more strongly about this now, and as I empower myself, I feel the need to empower other women to find their voices.

Whenever I look back at my mother and my grandmother, or women in general, they weren't treated with fairness. There was a lot of injustice.

I'm connecting those things now because I've seen how that affected my mother as an individual and a woman. Now, I'm taking the good things from my mum, such as the creative stuff, baking, her love of flowers—all her strengths. She was a great multitasker and carried the family, and I have taken that on. My mother was a great housekeeper, she was a great cook, and she loved her garden and nature.

In the search for truth human beings take two steps forward and one step back, suffering, mistakes and the weariness of life thrusts them back, but the thirst for truth will always drive you forwards again, and who knows, perhaps they or you will reach the real truth and you will be set free.

—Anton Chekhov

I'm writing this book because there is a pattern here: self-awareness, the spiritual aspect, letting go, and self-care. It's like a revolving circle. You must keep starting again and using what you learned from the last time around. You release the struggle and go back again, and something else will come up. The more self-aware you are, the more stuff will come up. The truth about healing is that it's not a destination—it's a journey.

Hurt people hurt people. That's how the pain pattern gets passed on generation after generation. Breaking the chain changes the future. This book is about liberation, and it's liberating me in the act of writing it for you, the person who reads it, to see that there is light at the end of the tunnel. For you, like me, there is a way through the pain and hurt that you may feel. I am not saying it's easy it takes courage. It involves moving from a place of victimhood to survivor to victor of your life.

CHAPTER 2

Ways of Connecting to Source

When I first reached out for help it was through hands-on healing—reiki. It balances out your system and the chakras that align up and down the body. When you have an emotional blockage, you feel it in your body. It may be a feeling of sadness, numbness, or depression. That could be a trigger that there is something for you to work on. Whatever is pushing the buttons, or whoever is pushing the buttons, there is an alarm going off. You know there is something that is not right, and you feel that you can't cope with it anymore.

It is usually some person in my life who is being my teacher. That person would have said or done something to me that presented some sort of difficulty, because it was related to a memory that I was not aware of. My husband was often my teacher. Things came up that I found stressful or difficult to deal with, and then I got into a pattern that when I got into that uncomfortableness, I took it to my healer. Whatever drama was being played out, she took me into the core of it. Whatever the core problem was, it came back to something that happened in childhood and created a memory.

It is like a session with a counsellor, but you get the feeling as well as the memory—how it felt for you at whatever stage of life it was at. I could see the picture of what was going on and how it made me feel. Then I released it and let it go.

That became a pattern for me throughout my journey. As I said earlier, when you took off that layer of the onion, it felt good for a while, but there is always another layer. There is always challenges in people's lives, but the challenge is there for a reason. It's highlighting that you're not taking care of yourself. Reiki is one way of going to get rid of that uncomfortableness. Reiki works, but it's not the only way.

Meditation

I use meditation on a daily basis. Because my life was so busy, it was good to take some time out to do a meditation exercise. The benefit of meditation is to reduce the stress, and it can give you clarity around your thoughts and feelings, as well as how you are as an individual. I bought CDs of meditation exercises that were twenty minutes or half an hour, and I found them very helpful.

Another way is to go out into nature and meditate outside, under a tree or beside a stream. A lot of meditation music is set in nature, so the best way to experience that is to be in nature. You are keeping your senses alert, and that dampens the thoughts.

You may focus on the water, perhaps a stream flowing by. It slows down the chitter-chatter of your thought process as you notice how the water flows, or how the leaves on the branches above your head move in the breeze. Listen to the water or the birds. If a thought comes, don't force it away. Simply let it come and let it go, like everything around you that is there for a moment and then gone. Let the stream take it away. If you don't want to be bombarded by thoughts, running water is a very good way to give your brain space.

Don't just think. Be here and present in the now. Enjoy whatever is in front of you—the running water or the birds or whatever noise you can hear. Listen and let go of the chitter-chatter that goes on in your head. It's a breathing space, a time-out space for you. You feel the peace. You're here and now in the present moment, enjoying what's in front of you. It creates a calmness.

Perhaps there is a place for you nearby that you have not yet discovered. Find it and make it your own. Once you immerse yourself in meditation in nature, you can come back to that place, either physically or in your imagination, at any time that you need to take the time out again.

If you don't yet have such a place, then a guided mediation on YouTube is a good substitute. You can also relax to music; piano or flute music is very good to switch off the chitter-chatter. You can choose whatever is right for you. It may not be right for everyone, but you can explore that area for yourself.

Walking in Nature

Every day I take myself off on a walk. If your head is muzzied with five or six different people coming at you, take yourself off for a fifteen-minute break with nature. If you don't take the time out, then I have learned eventually the stress will mount up. I need to take time out for me because I am no good to anybody else if I don't. Whenever I walk in nature, I feel alive and happy. It's my happy place, and it's because I know I am getting in touch with the source of everything.

Whenever you are connecting to source in this way, you are connecting to the energy of the universe. There is always a lot more going on around you than you can ever be aware of. You realise that you are not the centre of everything. You are a part of a bigger picture, but you feel part of it, and you feel very small at the same time. You do have a part to play and a purpose.

Every little thing has an effect; there is such a connection between our lives and the lives of trees and animals. They can teach us so much. Take the trunk of a tree and its roots. I find trees fascinating. They draw the negative energy out of you. If you spend just fifteen minutes walking beneath trees, by the time you come out the other end, you will be more positive. If you put your hands on a tree, you can feel its energy flowing up from the roots, and your own energy becomes grounded, connected to the earth. You become more centred and balanced as an individual. That's how you can find your balance if you are feeling stressed or out of sorts.

When I first started walking, I didn't realise what was going on, but the more I did it, the more it became part of my conscious spiritual practice. I have gotten to the stage now that I build it into my life as a regular daily exercise. I create time for it, and if I don't do it for two days, then I know that I am missing part of my self-care, and I need to do it.

Journaling

Journaling is a tool that clarifies your thoughts and feelings. Pay attention to your feelings, and uncomfortable feelings in particular; they will tell you a lot. Your soul speaks to you in feelings. Listen to them because they have important messages for you.

Normally, I would sit down with a book and a pen every day, and I talk to myself. I write myself a question, or I write one word, and before I know it, I have a page written. It's a great way to express your thoughts, your feelings, and whatever is going on in your head. Once you get it on paper, it becomes real. Every day you sit down to write, you will write something different.

It's good to start with a question, even if it is 'How are you feeling today?' or 'What do you want me to do today?' just as if you are talking to someone else. Then you listen and write down whatever comes to you. Whatever the answer is, write it down. I find it gives me great clarity about what is my next move. What should I be doing, or where do I need to go, or to whom do I need to talk? What's next on my path?

I find journaling is a wonderful way to get rid of worries and concerns and to reconnect with my intuition. I feel like I am connecting with source as I begin to have amazing ideas, inspiration, and realisations.

I also use a gratitude journal at night. Before I go to sleep, I list perhaps five things that I could be grateful for. I believe that when you are grateful, it opens the way to find more things to be grateful for. As a society I think we have lost a bit of that; but it must come from yourself – it can't come from other people telling you what to be grateful for. There might not actually be more things, but you notice them more; you really begin to appreciate what is in your life. If you are in a bad place and you do five things that you are grateful for, sometimes it can get things into perspective.

Yoga

Yoga is great way of being aware of what is going on in your body. If you regularly go to yoga, you are letting go of pain; you are letting go of the stiffness within your body, so it doesn't build up over time.

Yoga works on the whole body. The different yoga poses work on different organs, moving, releasing, and letting go so that there is a better chance your body won't get into a state where you take an illness. When you find that emotions get stuck in some organ, your body will tell you. If you have uncomfortable feelings about something, it helps you to stay with that feeling and not suppress it, until you can release it and let it go. If you have a disease or your body is not at ease, it will let you know in some way if you simply listen.

Each part of the body is related to some sort of problem that you have in your life, or to a certain emotion. For example, the lower back is related to finances. If you have pain in your body, there is always an underlying reason for that pain. It may be an old injury, but there may be some other some reason why it has come up again at that particular time.

Reflexology

Throughout my years, I would have held stress in my shoulders, and I went regularly to reflexology. Reflexology works on your feet. Every part of your foot is related to an organ in your body. If you have knots or stress elsewhere, then they feel it in your feet and work out the gritty bits, as I call them. Again, it helps you feel more alive, more balanced, and more able to cope with life.

Dance

When I did my diploma in healing, I went to dancing one night a week for a full year. If you sat in a chair from Monday to Sunday and didn't do any sort of movement, your brain would start to suffer. To have good health, you need to keep your body and your mind active. If you keep moving, you keep moving the stress out of your life. You keep renewing your spirit, shifting, and letting go.

Vision Boards

The vision board is a great way to think about what you need to do or be in your life. It is like the mood boards used by designers. Take a pile of magazines or other sources and pull out whatever words and images appeal to you. Do not ask at this stage why the image appeals. When you have enough, place them on a board and move them around, adding and subtracting until you are happy with the arrangement. I would incorporate a meditation exercise here, to get yourself centred and in a good space. Then take the words and images and put together a board. It's a very personal thing. Whenever people do it, it's their stuff—what they are bringing out and putting on paper. It's focussing on how they want to be, what they want to have, and what they want to do.

I find that if you have total peace and quiet before you do a vision board, you can get into the zone. Every picture or every word on that board is right. Don't think too much about it; simply let it come. Something will resonate with you, and once you have your images spread all over the floor, just start to put them on the board. It's exactly as it should be, in a sense.

It's good to do these on a regular basis because it changes over time. I know I've looked at vision boards that I have done in the past and realised three months down the line that I had achieved what was on that vision board, so it was time to do a new one.

Here's an example of a vision board I did some time ago.

The very top bit is saying yes to my favourite things and then asking myself how I can use those favourite things to help people make small steps so they also can let go of their past. Forgiveness is the key to letting go. The more you let go, the more you surrender, and the more you heal your hurt and your pain, eventually you arrive at happiness and health, and you achieve inner peace. That is exactly what I want out of my book.

Then around that are my own favourite things. Flowers are important, I think because of colour. The more colour you have in your life, the brighter your life is. Your food also represents colour. For example, if you have on your plate all the different colours of fruits and vegetables. It's nourishment for your mind, your body, and your soul.

Mabel Campbell

Foraging

I do this whilst I walk. There's so much that you can take from nature. At each time of the year, nature presents us with an abundance of something different. For example, in December you can forage for greenery, holly, and stuff like that. You can bring the outside in, and it affects your environment. I would use greenery to make a centrepiece for my table. It's using what you've got, using your creativity with those bits and pieces.

Journaling, escaping the rat race, and getting away from it all are essential to our health and well-being. We should take ourselves out of the hustle and bustle, particularly at Christmas.

It's all about using the countryside to improve your own health and well-being and live well. That could be growing your own flowers, herbs, fruits, and vegetables. Flowers have an amazing effect. Each flower represents something. If you are attracted to a particular colour, it corresponds to a chakra in your body that wants healing. At different times of your life, you might be attracted to purple, for example, which is for enlightenment and your crown chakra.

Walking and the use of your hands in growing your own food are things that people always have always done. The meditation, the journaling, and the reflexology are all techniques. I think I was drawn to each of them because they could help me, and they did. I can share only what I have used because I have proved that they have worked for me, but it is all based on learning to love yourself, and when you know that, you have the means to heal.

CHAPTER 3

Self-Care

Self-care and self-love is a practice that you can learn to incorporate into your everyday life.

> *Owning our story and loving ourselves through that process is the bravest thing that we'll ever do*
>
> —Brené Brown

Self-care is really important if you are embarking on this journey of finding your true self. Taking care of yourself is never a selfish act. Self-care is an action you take for yourself to say, 'I love you, I appreciate you, and you are important.'

Our bodies, minds, and emotions keep us informed as to whether they are being taken care of in the way they need to be. A self-care plan is broken down into four categories: physical, mental/emotional, social, and spiritual.

Physical Self-Care

Physical self-care includes activities and practices such as exercise and healthy eating. When you exercise, your body releases chemicals called endorphins, which boost your mood and reduce stress. Take note of what you are eating. The food we eat affects our energy, our mood, and our sleep.

Physical self-care also means the physical environment in which we live. Your outer environment is a reflection of what's going on inside. When your environment is cluttered and messy, you may have overwhelming and stressful clutter inside as well.

I do not indulge as much as I once did, but throughout my life, I used food as an emotional comfort. That had been a pattern for me. If I didn't know how to express my emotions, I would go to the cupboard for biscuits or other sweet stuff. A lot of people aren't aware that when you eat sweet stuff, it can become an addiction because your body craves more of it. It becomes a vicious circle. You get your sugar high, but when you come down, you crave more of it.

I had to go on a low-glycaemic diet advocated by Patrick Holford to balance my sugar levels. It is based on the concept of combining foods. For example, if you eat a carbohydrate, you should balance it with a protein at the same time. If you eat an apple, you should eat some nuts with it. What I do now for snacks is use oatcakes or maybe hummus instead of reaching for the biscuits. You get a slower release of sugar into your bloodstream, so you are not looking for something else soon after.

For the past three or four months, I have also been off meat. I have no idea why. Now I am eating a plant-based diet, and I find I have more energy. I noticed it this Christmas. I have a family of four kids, their partners, and their kids, so there was quite a lot of cooking. I didn't get as tired as I normally did. Apart from diet, I also put that down to the walking and other exercise that I do, as well as drinking a lot more water.

If you eat mainly vegetables, it doesn't mean that you have to be starved of 'nice food'. There are lots of things that you can do. When I am cooking for a lot of people, I base it around onions, mushrooms, and vegetables, and then I have rice or quinoa. I would do it all in one pan, and then I would separate it and add the meat for whoever wants meat. In mine, I would have kidney beans or red beans. I eat a lot of black beans, kidney beans, and chickpeas. You can even make up a burger with chickpeas, and if you are cooking a burger, you can cook it alongside meat burgers. It's not difficult, and it encourages the family to think about what they are eating. I've heard them commenting over Christmas that they would have eaten less of the sweet stuff as well—and felt better for it. You're not pushing it in their faces, but you do have an impact simply by making little adjustments for yourself.

Decluttering

Decluttering with intention can be a spiritual practice and can bring great joy as part of this journey. Clutter represents stagnant energy. It keeps you in the past, encourages procrastination, and makes you feel tired, overwhelmed, confused, angry, stuck, and depressed. Decluttering is part of the letting go process; when we are no longer controlled by clutter, we grow and change in ways that brings us closer to God. Decluttering helps us focus on what's important in our household. It shines a light in what's getting in the way of living life. As you shift clutter and let go of what's not needed, new opportunities await.

In the home, the kitchen is a symbol of how we care for ourselves and our bodies, as well as the way we treat our resources (food and money). The kitchen represents your wealth and also your deepest self. As you clean and polish your kitchen, you are cleansing and polishing your inner self and your emotions. The kitchen can illustrate a lack of emotional support and self-control. If you are ready to take back your personal power, then decluttering the kitchen is a good place to start.

If you have clutter in your garage, you may have difficulty moving forward in life. Remove clutter in this area if you want to feel liberated and free. The attic symbolises our connection to the past, our families and ancestors, and our higher selves. When you fill your attic with unwanted items, you literally have stuff hanging over your head that can make it difficult to resolve issues from your past. You are holding on to their beliefs and their ways of doing things. When I started the healing process, my attic was full of crap. Once I started to let go of stuff in my head, I gutted the whole of my attic. Now, all that is there is seasonal stuff such as the Christmas tree.

Pick up items in your home one at a time and ask

yourself, 'Does this spark joy in me?' If the answer is no, thank it for its time with you and discard it.

There is a great deal to be said for simplicity. If you have a wardrobe bursting with clothes, you can't see the forest for the trees. There is no point in holding on to stuff that you are not wearing.

Try this: Keep all clothes of the same type together, either hanging on a rail or folded in a drawer in a row, so that they are all visible. Whenever you need something to wear, take the first suitable item from the right. When you are done with it, place it back on the left, moving everything else along. After a while, all the clothes you never wear are on the right, and you can then decide what to do with them. If you haven't worn it for a year, it's time to let it go. It's not serving you. You are holding on to scarcity, or the fear that you don't have enough money to buy new clothes. Once you let go, the money will come to buy new stuff, and you can be quite clear about what you need to buy. Be specific so that what you buy has a purpose.

I have used the process of decluttering throughout my spiritual journey. Things like paperwork build up. They can build up unnoticed. The simple process of decluttering brings clarity and sometimes points out symbolic meaning. For example, I got the brake pads replaced on the front of my car. What might that mean? Braking up, pulling back? Your car is part of your body, so if there is a part of your car that keeps breaking down for no obvious reason, that may also be a sign of something you haven't noticed in your body or your life.

Your house is the same. Your washing machine, your pipes, or maybe the sewers in your house. If they block, then perhaps it's teaching you that you need to let go. Just before Christmas, I repainted my kitchen and cleaned it all out. That was before I started to eat better, more plant-based food. I think the very fact of cleaning the kitchen made me think more about what I was eating. It may work the other way too. If you change your diet, you may look at all the things in your ladder and think, 'Do I need these?'

When I do my groceries now, I make sure that there are a lot of fruit and vegetables. In my cupboards, there are very few processed meals. I don't buy those because I know that it lowers my energy vibration.

This cleaning and decluttering even applies to your windows. If I need to see more clearly, I get an urge to clean my windows and take away the dirt. Everything has a symbolic meaning. It might not be the same for other people, but that's how it is for me. As with reading poetry or fiction, you may understand that something stands for something else. Someone else doesn't see it, but you know it's there.

That's the effect of decluttering; if you clear out your environment and open the windows to let in the light, you see what else can be changed. I go into houses where the blinds are closed, and if I was living in that house, I would feel claustrophobic. I'm always looking out, and I'm always looking how I can improve and evolve. These people are closing themselves away from the world, and I don't want to be like that. I want to be out there!

Emotional Self-Care

Listen to your own body and what you need. It's not being selfish—it's taking care of you so that you can take care of others. Sometimes you need to take the time out so you can come back better. You need to find what is best for yourself. From your upbringing and your learned patterns, it may be that you over-give to the point of exhaustion. If you are not aware of how you are feeling, you can turn it around and become resentful. You can moan and complain and blame everyone else for what you are putting yourself through.

> *When you blame and criticise others you are avoiding some truth about yourself*
>
> —Deepak Chopra

The important thing is to get the balance right and know that once you have had enough of something, you can pull back and take yourself out of it.

Social Self-Care

Social needs include the need for belonging, love, and affection. Life passes too quickly, but your family and friends are important. Take time for them, or join a club where you can connect and engage with people.

I noticed over Christmas that when there were people about the house, they would come in and moan about their work. Sometimes people do want help, but sometimes they simply want to drag you into their own drama, so you get sucked into criticising the people with whom they are working—people whom you don't even know.

Now, I simply hold my own space and let people ramble. Maybe that's not a good way to explain it, but if you get sucked into the drama, then your energy becomes depleted. You become the exhausted person, and they go home on a high.

You must set yourself a boundary. Recognise what is going on with other people. All that negative energy will go somewhere, and if you're not careful, you will end up with it.

I keep telling my kids, 'Don't let other people steal your joy.' It's not dishonouring the person or disrespecting the person, but it's knowing what you can change, if in fact you can change anything. If you can't change others, you simply have to send them good wishes and hand it over to God to deal with. You can offer suggestions for how people can change, but if they are not hearing you or are not in a place themselves where they want to take ownership or responsibility, then you have to let them be.

I need my own space. It's part of who I am; I need the peace and the quiet. I find myself coming back to that time and time again. If there is busyness going on, you need to take your time out of it. It's not good to isolate yourself either, because if you do that, you tend to overthink things. I have been thinking about what is next for me and how I can incorporate my self-care into that. In my diary, I need to schedule me time. If you don't, you can be sucked back into giving up all your time. You need to be able to recognise—the whole self-awareness thing—that you need to take the time out to receive as well.

Spiritual Self-Care

Spiritual self-care is about peeling back the layers and really getting to know your true essence, your soul. It helps you to connect with that still point within, which you find in meditation. Each element of your self-care plan is dependent on the others for a proper life balance.

The Serenity Prayer

God, grant me the serenity to accept the things I cannot change, courage to change the things I can, and the wisdom to know the difference

There are three parts to the serenity prayer.

In other words, we're asking God for three things: serenity, courage, and wisdom.

Serenity has its time and place, courage has its time and place, and wisdom is the ability to know whether it's a time and place for serenity or for courage.

For example, in a situation where we are convinced that if we simply try harder, come on stronger, and give things another chance, it may be because of our perfectionist drive to control people, places, and things. We believe that reality ought to be different than it is, and therefore we are sure we just need more git and gumption to see things through. However, what we really need is the ability to let go and let God. We don't need courage in that situation, but serenity.

I find myself going back to the serenity prayer quite a lot, particularly in my extended family circle. The more I see, the more I believe that people must take responsibility for themselves as individuals, even with regards to their own health.

Church

People can change their values over time. I grew up within the norm of attending church and Sunday school on a regular basis, going on to be a Sunday school teacher. We were taught in church that God is up there in the sky. We are also taught a lot about fear—that if we don't abide by the rules of the church, we won't get to heaven. I took myself out of church as I went along my personal journey. I felt this need to explore, and I found that we were preached to instead of learning from an experimental concept. I also felt that the church was full of power-hungry attitudes and people who used their egos to control others through the fear they taught.

Today, I feel I don't need to be attached to a church. This may change in the future; I don't know. I have realised that God has been beside me all the time. God is within. The world needs to wake up and hear this. God is not about rules and fear. God is not up there in the sky. God is within you and me.

> *But the fruit of the Spirit is 'love, joy, peace, patience, kindness, goodness, faithfulness, gentleness and self-control.'*
>
> (Galatians 5:22–23)

God didn't create religion; men did. We are all one—one with God and one with life. Change happens in the world if we come from a place of love.

Chapter 4

Letting Go

Look at where you are at and what is happening in your life. Now think about what you need to let go of. What is causing you stress? The more you can let go, the more peace you will have, and the more freedom you will have within yourself.

I used to belong to different organisations, giving and giving and going out almost every day, exhausting myself. When my kids were growing up, I would be on a lot of different committees, to the point where I was burning out. There's usually a reason for doing something like that; in my case, I was looking for approval outside of myself. It all goes to show how important self-awareness and self-reflection is. You need to decide what you want from yourself.

We can waste so many years of our lives. I would sit and watch people going for a walk. I'd see them with their heads down, and I wondered what was pressing on them. You never really know what is going on in another person's life. I've been there, and I'm used to do it. Life is to be enjoyed,

Remembering Who I am

and if you get sucked into the idea that life is a struggle, that's what you are going to get.

If you worry about it, you push it away, but if you trust, you will always be provided for. If you worry, you are not actually living life—you are struggling. Once you let go of all the bunkum and the baggage that you carry, you can start to create new patterns of learned behaviour. The more you let go, the more you trust yourself. If you are presented with a challenge, the challenge is there to help you grow. You will take something out of it, so embrace it!

Healing is hard, but the process of letting go will have an immense impact on your life. It takes courage to change, but it begins by recognising the uncomfortableness in the way you are trying to live. That's a sign that you need to let go of something. It takes work to get that monkey off your back, but the more you can take off, the more peace you will have in your life. It brings freedom. If you think about it, the opposite of fear is freedom. If you let go of the fear, the pain, and the sadness, you will become freer—but you must do the work. There's no use in simply wishing.

The worst thing that anyone can do is to pretend that it's OK. I've met people who are so jolly, coming out with jokes all the time. Sometimes that's a coping mechanism. Reach out and find someone you can connect with who can help you. When you come up against a block, you will have that one person to whom you can go back to.

Finding joy, peace of mind, a fulfilling life, living in the moment, love, faith, forgiveness, spiritual growth, and moving beyond negative emotions means taking responsibility for your life. It's the hope of every living person on this planet, but it requires time, strength, and courage.

This process involves letting go of the old beliefs we have about ourselves, life, and the world around us. This process is ongoing, but it is the single most powerful step that you can do towards starting to create a life that you desire.

If we let go a little, we have a little peace.

If we let go a lot, we have a lot of peace

If we let go completely, we have complete peace

—Ajahn Chah

Letting go is an evolving process throughout the healing journey. As you move on and listen, pay attention to what is presenting itself—the uncomfortableness. As you work on that, it brings in the process of letting go. The uncomfortable feeling is a signal that something is wrong. There is something triggering it, and you need to work on the reason why. There is always a reason. It may be something that you can't work out yourself, but it keeps repeating itself so that you keep attracting the same situation. You need to take the courage to look at it. You realise that it is there to teach you; there is something at a deeper level with which you need to heal.

A healer can take you into that deeper memory. Sometimes that can be painful to look at, but if you know and trust that you are being guided, you can examine the emotions around it.

Dealing with Childhood Trauma

Usually a situation triggers a memory through something that has gone on in your childhood which has affected your learned pattern of belief. You usually get a picture of some sort of a memory. There is a correlation between that picture and what is going on in your life. It may have something to do with abuse, physical, emotional or sexual, or it may be an argument that you overheard between your mum and your dad.

You were in the middle of it as a child, and you didn't know how to cope with it then. You take on that pattern. You thought that it was your responsibility or your fault, even though you were a child. One wee memory can have such an impact on you. You did not understand the situation, so you took on your parents' pattern of dealing with it. When you can look at it for yourself now, with adult eyes, you can connect with it let it go. You understand why you react that way, and you realise that you don't have to continue reacting the same way in future.

First, you must get in touch with the feeling, the emotion. You must feel it again, but not in a bad way. You must admit to yourself that that's how you felt at that time. Perhaps you were only three years old, and you couldn't have done any different. You didn't understand what was going on, and it wasn't your fault. Abuse happens within families, and until somebody breaks the cycle, it will continue to happen. Once you go to healing, you start to break that link. Once you deal with the abuse through the healing process, you take back your power. Abuse robs you of your power; as a child, you don't have the self-awareness to understand what happened.

After I got married and began raising my own kids, that experience brought up the memories for me. When I was working with the victims of the Troubles and dealing with their traumas, that also triggered more trauma. As you look at the difficult issues that are presenting in your everyday life, you come to see the reasons why you are behaving the way you are as an adult.

For example, I was an angry person, but I didn't connect it to my childhood, so I projected the anger out. Once I started to look at my sexual abuse, I was able to see that I was blaming myself. The person who abused me was an adult; I was a child, but I had suppressed it, thinking this was normal and I must be to blame for how I was feeling. I didn't have the awareness back then to realise that it wasn't normal. I would become angry whenever I was under pressure or stress, and I didn't know why. I didn't have the proper coping mechanisms until I started to deal with the memories and the trauma, and then my anger started to subside.

When I see someone being abusive to someone else now, I find I have my voice to speak out about it. Previously I was suppressed, and I had lost my power. Within a family situation, how you speak to people shows how much power you really have. If you shout and roar, there's always a reason for that behaviour. If you are not dealing with people in a respectful manner, your behaviour is crossing a boundary, and you need to draw back and ask yourself why you are speaking in that way. You need to connect your present behaviour with what has gone on with yourself as a child.

Once you go back and deal with the memory of the abuse that you have suffered—whether it is physical, sexual, or emotional abuse—the behaviour sorts itself out. You don't need to be angry anymore because you have taken back your power and putting the blame where it should be.

Knowledge is power. You create an understanding of it so you can release it and let it go. You can accept that it happened, but you realise that it was not your fault, so you don't have to beat yourself up about it anymore. You don't need to struggle with it or sabotage yourself. Abuse can put a terrible burden of shame on you as an adult because that's how a child internalises it. Unless people deal with it in an adult way and the effects that it is causing in their life, it can rob them of a joyful life.

Forgiveness

As the Lord's Prayer says, "Forgive us our sins, as we forgive those who sin against us."

First, you need to forgive yourself. In my circumstances, I was looking for attention, for love, because I didn't know what it was.

You need to forgive yourself, but you also need to forgive

the perpetrators. That doesn't mean to say that what they did wasn't wrong, or that they should not be brought to justice if that is possible. However, if you do not forgive, then you are still holding on to the wrong that they have done you. If you continue to blame people, it's not harming them in any way—it's you whom it harms. You must eventually come to the point where you can say, 'OK, this has happened to me, and it was wrong, but I am done taking responsibility.'

This is where the healing process comes in. You accept that there is a higher power working through, and that's God. You will eventually realise that it is God helping you to release and let it go. There is a massive power in that. You must believe that you can be healed. You can get better. You can release whatever it is you have been carrying around.

When I started to go to healing, it felt like a massive weight on my shoulders, like a four-stone bag of potatoes. You have had that on your back for several years, but you start by taking one potato out, and another potato out, until the bag is empty. Can you imagine what it feels like then? You get in touch with your real core, and then you start to create your life again.

Letting Go of the Future

As well as memories of the past, you may be burdened by fears for the future. Perhaps you have a fear about not having enough money.

This is where God comes in again; you must trust the universe will supply. The more you focus on your lack of money or whatever, the more experiences of lack you will attract. When that sort of fear comes up, I look for something positive to replace it with, and I dwell on that. You need to focus on where you want to go, not on what you want to avoid. That's where your self-awareness comes in again. You can get on a merry-go-round of fear and avoidance until you realise, 'I've been here before. I need to do something different.' You need to explore what took you back there and how you will deal with it. You have to say to yourself, 'That's not the way I want to live my life. This is the way I want to live my life.' It's useful to have a mantra, a phrase you can repeat as a way to remind yourself of that. Then you need to act on what you are telling yourself to do; otherwise, you will keep attracting more of the wrong stuff.

Letting Go of the Need to Prove Yourself

If you are constantly looking for approval outside yourself, there is lack of love for yourself. Once you start to love yourself, you don't need approval from outside because you get it there. That's where you find your sense of self and build it up again. You are the best person to decide whether you have done the best that you could.

Letting Go of Relationships

Different forms of abuse will attract different people into your life. You can become dependent on relationships unless you start to take responsibility for yourself. When your actions and thoughts revolve around another person to the complete disregard of your own individuality, this is what's called co-dependency. Sometimes you can get so involved in other people's plans that you need to pull back and realise, 'This is their baby, not mine.' Co-dependency is harmful; a healthy relationship is one that doesn't try to change you or control you.

Friends and family won't always support your personal journey, but carry on anyhow. Following your intuition means doing what is right for you, even if it doesn't sound right for others. We all have our individual paths to lead.

Letting Go of Fear

Fear is the root cause of control issues. When you are afraid, you want to get back to the security of things that you know you can control. Whether you blame others or become dependent on others, you give up your power to change. Not taking responsibility can be less demanding, less painful, and more comfortable, but there is always a price to pay.

> *Within every setback or obstacle you encounter there is a seed of an equal or greater advantage or benefit. Find it.*
>
> —Brian Tracey

Life begins at the end of your comfort zone. Once you step out of that place where everything is known and predictable, you begin to get in touch with your real self. Discipline yourself to do what you know is right and important. Seek out help. For years, I thought when I asked for help, it was a sign of weakness. I soon learnt that asking for help shows strength and bravery, and it's an act of self-love.

Getting Help

Don't go it alone. Pride is a big thing in our society—the idea that you need to man up and pretend that you don't need help. That's a learned belief from society, and it has a great effect upon your mental health. Mental health is so much of a stigma that we don't want to talk about it, but surely it takes more courage to man up and tell your story so that you can get help. People are trying to deal with their own stuff, but we need each other.

When I went into social farming, I was stepping well outside my comfort zone. I was going into a world that I knew very little about, but I liked the concept because it sat well with my values. I trusted that I would know what I was doing when the time came and that help would be there when I needed it.

Looking for help is a sign of strength. It shows you where you want to go and that you are not getting there by your own efforts alone. You want to live life, not just cope with it. Coping with life—telling yourself that everything will work out OK so long as it just keeps going on and nothing changes—is telling yourself a lie. Sooner or later, things will change in ways you can't control. Taking that first step to reach out for help is a sign that you have the courage to want to change.

Letting go is the inner action that removes the fear, upset, and tunnel vision. The moment you let go, you restore your ability to see clearly. You become more creative and are able to discover solutions to your problems that you had never seen before.

> *The greatest prison people live in is the fear of what other people think.*
>
> —David Icke

Remember that fear is a state of mind, and it is created by resistance. The more you resist, the bigger the fear will become. For fear to lose its power, do the opposite of what creates it.

Sometimes during the healing process, you start to think, 'Why me?' and you want to blame God for giving you all this stuff. It takes a while to work out that God has a purpose. Each one of us has a purpose on Earth, and we are here to work it out. Some people believe that if you don't learn all you have to learn in this life, your spirit will come back in another body and keep repeating until it has learnt the lesson. If that is the case, then perhaps the people who have an easy life are still in kindergarten.

As you engage more in the process of letting go, you will

crave more time to be alone. Solitude provides an opportunity to reflect, feel your true power emerging, and find your own voice. Solitude provides time to provide answers to your problems more quickly. Solitude can enhance the quality of your relationships; you're more likely to make better choices about who you want to be around. Solitude is an essential part of your self-care plan.

For years I feared being alone and clung to other people. I have learnt the hard way. Question your beliefs on this one. Gradually, as you get used to being alone, you will become OK with it. You will come to love it.

Be gentle with yourself. In some ways, letting go is a mourning process. You are losing the person you once were, with all of your old certainties. It is the death of who you thought you were. Perhaps you had a fantasy of who you could be if only 'they' would let you, or you fantasises about the perfect family that you should have had.

When you peel it all back, the reality hits home. You will never be that person. You have been building that fantasy in order to cope with your life. It's a fantasy because you were not seriously working to make it come true.

If by any chance it might come true, you would have found a way to sabotage it, because you didn't want your dream crushed by reality.

If you suppress that sadness, it may lead to depression. Under depression, there is obviously anger that your dreams are frustrated, and under anger, there is sadness, and under the sadness there is usually guilt. Guilt for what?

> *Forgive yourself for not knowing what you didn't know before you lived through it. Honour your path. Trust your journey. Learn, grow, evolve and become.*
>
> —Creig Crippen

When you get past that point, you may want to consider a silent retreat, as is now offered in more and more places. Creating quiet time alone for yourself is the key to becoming the best version of yourself. Time alone develops awareness of the people in your life and whether they contribute to your positive energy. Time alone gives you the strength and wisdom to say no to anyone or anything that makes you unhappy.

I have suffered a lot through physical, sexual, and emotional abuse, and now, sitting here today, I am so grateful to have been myself through all that. From here, it can only get better. Once you get your purpose, you have to keeping remembering it. Keep remembering who you are and why you are who you are.

The first step in letting go is to trust. Trust that you will be OK no matter what happens. Even if your greatest fears come true, know that you will be fine.

The second part of letting go is to be willing to feel your hurt of unsolved issues.

The key to releasing the hurt is to feel it like a child. Let it come and let it go. Continue to seek help for this process.

> Know that problems are as a result of feeling separate from God. Learn to get into touch with the silence within yourself and know that everything in life has a purpose. There are no mistakes, no coincidences, all events are blessings given to us to learn from.
>
> —Elisabeth Kubler-Ross

CHAPTER 5

Spiritual Surrender

You've tried everything and still aren't where you want to be. So give up the struggle and let life move through you with spiritual surrender

—Sally Kempton

I struggled from a very young age. I was raised in the belief that if I didn't work hard and achieve, the solution was to work even harder. This had detrimental effects on my health. I put everyone's needs before my own, leaving myself exhausted and resentful at times. I have learnt the value of spiritual surrender the hard way. It has taken me a long time to realise the great and mysterious truth of who or what is really in charge. It's clearer to me that each time I surrender—that is, stop struggling for a certain result, release the control freak that I once was, and place everything in the hands of the higher power—doors open both in the inner and outer worlds. You return to oneness with the Great Divine, and surrender brings peace that you won't find any other way.

Surrender does not mean giving up. True surrender is always to the higher, deeper will and the life force itself. It's a way of being.

If you surrender attachment to a particular outcome, things often turn out better than you could ever imagined.

Surrender is the key to unlocking anxiety and fear.

Surrender is becoming aware of God's energy within oneself, recognising that energy, and accepting it.

Surrender requires practice in turning over difficult situations that you don't feel you have the capacity to handle to the universe, to the higher power that is God.

You have a choice to allow it or resist it. What we resist persists. For this to work, it requires you to enter a deep sense of trust. Let your energy take you where it knows you're meant to go. Start loving the world and life, relax, feel love at your heart, and keep focusing on that in every situation you encounter.

There are three steps to spiritual surrender: pray, let go, and listen.

Pray

Ask for manifestation of the greatest good for your life. Ask for support. Ask for help in letting go of any fear you may have. Remember that challenges come up to help you grow and to show you areas where there is lack of internal harmony.

For example, maybe your family doesn't understand your spiritual growth and your awakening, and this causes you stress. Surrender your outcome to God, to your higher self. Give yourself the space, self-love, and care you need to stand within your power—and ask the Divine to step in.

If you are trying to manifest something, then yes, surrender it to the Divine, but remember that action is also needed if you are so prompted.

Listen to your inner guidance, listen to your intuition. Trust yourself.

Faith is like a muscle: you strengthen it through constant practice.

Ask yourself these questions.
- Where would you have me to go?
- What would you have me to do?
- What would you have me to say? And to whom?

Let Go

Spiritual surrender means surrendering to life and to a greater power, which you will find out is your true self. Spiritual surrender means letting go of everything—yourself included.

The final letting go is letting go of all the ideas you have about yourself and all the things you want yourself to be and become, even the new ones that you are most excited about. Whatever is meant to stay will stay. Relax into that when you get to this place. Relax into trusting that life knows how to express itself without even your help. The purpose of life in this moment is to stop trying to control it.

This is what life is now, and no one knows what tomorrow will bring. That's freedom.

This is what life is right now. This is how life expresses itself through you right now. How will it express itself tomorrow? I haven't got a clue!

True surrender means letting your mind be emptied from all concepts and beliefs. Let go of them all. Let the mind get quiet and cleaned out. This is how it feels to really love your life; it's prefect and beautiful.

Surrender means letting go of everything you thought yourself to be and what you believed life was about. Let life itself live and express itself through you.

Listen

As you journey on your path, you will come across some difficult periods, but as you overcome your challenges, you move on to bigger and better things. Like climbing a mountain, the path becomes steeper and more challenging as you go on, but the rewards are also greater.

When you reach the peak, you can take a deep sigh of relief and enjoy the expansive view of the world below. You get to see things from a higher perspective. You begin to see life the way God sees things. You see the wisdom in God's plan, and because you are a piece of God, you are part of the plan. You become the observer in life, not the helpless victim.

There are some many areas of growth that we can focus on in our lives. We are here to enjoy abundance, and to develop our spiritual nature. My experience on this journey hasn't exactly been an easy one. There have been many pitfalls along the way. You may fall off a cliff and tumble down the mountain. The important thing to remember is to never give up. Pick yourself up and keep climbing. You will be a wiser person for having experienced the pitfalls and challenges that life throws at you. The key is to remember to turn inward time and time again for the answers. When you come to the end of your life's journey, everything will make sense, and you will get to celebrate coming home to your true home.

CHAPTER 6

The Essence of Who You Are

Your essence is your soul, or your higher self. It is not the stories (good or bad) that you tell about yourself; it is what you have come here to know. If you think about all your years of growing up and what you have gathered from culture, from society, from family, all your education, and your experiences, that is not your essence. It's there, but it doesn't define you. You can detach from it. I believe that your soul has come from somewhere else, and it will go on to somewhere else, but it has something to learn in this life. You are a child of God.

There are times when you have to stand back and ask yourself, 'Have I, as an individual, become separate from my higher self, my soul? Have I forgotten what I have come here for?'

Learning

Every person is here to learn something. You are here for a purpose, and you have a choice whether to follow that purpose or to drift through life. It's not the same for everyone; a lot of people might never find what their purpose is on Earth, or they might not even be interested.

I have always been a seeker. There is something driving me. I have always been looking for that purpose, and that small inner voice has been nudging me to learn more and understand more of who I am. That might not be for everybody, but I feel you may be another seeker. If you can connect with what I am trying to get across, that will take you a wee bit further on your journey.

I think the essence is a matter of being whole and complete while going forward in pursuit of that purpose you have found for yourself. It's being authentic; you come in alignment with where you need to go. When you get knocked off, remembering who you are brings you back into alignment, into reality. Your higher self-centres you, and that's where you find your peace. The more you let go of your baggage, the less you drift away, and the more quickly you realise that you can come back to that centre place. Self-awareness and self-reflection help you. You start to use your learning to reinforce your understanding. The challenges come up so that you can look at where you are going and understand it more deeply.

Your essence sets your course for you. No one else can set it for you. It's always been there to set your course, and if you go off at a tangent, you always have the control to bring it back.

When you are young or inexperienced, you may not have a clear picture of who you are. As you get older, you use the wisdom of your learning. You come to an aha moment when you get a feeling of 'That's what it's all about'.

Sometimes it's a realisation: 'I don't need to be doing this.' You find you can let go of an old pattern of behaviour that has not been serving you. Recognising your essence shows you that you have so much potential, and it can only be good. It won't be perfect, but as you face the same things again, you will find that it is easier. You will find that there were experiences that you went through in the past which seemed to have no reason at the time, yet suddenly you see how they relate to your current life.

You learn the truth of your life, the truth of you. The more experiences that you encounter and the more you pay attention, the more you grow. You have come full circle, yet you have moved on, so you are not in the same place, and you do not have to react in the same way.

Joy

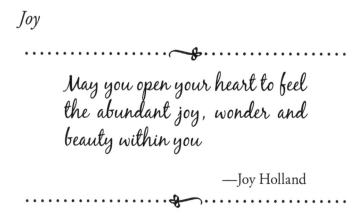

May you open your heart to feel the abundant joy, wonder and beauty within you

—Joy Holland

Joy is your birthright. You are love and light. Love yourself first, because that's who you'll be spending the rest of your life with.

There are many ways that you can increase your joy. Decide each week to take a trip to somewhere that makes your heart sing. It could be the ocean, the cinema, or a fine restaurant. Try your hand at something new, or go somewhere nice in nature. Ask yourself this question every morning: 'How can I bring joy into my life today?'

One person's joy is not another's, and you will discover for yourself what brings you joy. Be open to new experiences because where you find joy is where you will find your true self.

When you find what brings you joy, then mould it into something that you can share with others. That will bring you to a place where you can become more grounded and more at peace with your higher self. It's good to step outside your comfort zone. It gives you potential to grow in new directions, but that growth will always be rooted in the core of who you are. You will find that the new experience resonates with your core value system. If it does not, it is a distraction; let it go.

Throughout your day, remember to not let anything or anyone steal your joy. If you feel a situation is stealing your joy, you should stop, think, and refocus. You have the power to turn that around. You can choose to not let it steal your joy. Remember that joy is found in stillness. Joy will always come from within.

Trust

You are going to come up against challenging situations no matter where you are or who you are with. You can begin to fear or to worry, but if it is truly out of your control, you need to trust. This is where you come back to the serenity Prayer: if it's out of your control, hand it over to your higher self or God. Remember the law of attraction: the more you worry, the more you will find to worry about.

That is a big thing that I had to learn. You do have a choice: to keep worrying, or to trust. If you can change the situation, it's OK to do it. But if you can't, why are you worrying?

If you are at a crossroads, that is a good place to be. There may be some new direction that you haven't considered yet. Be still and wait for it to reveal itself.

You need patience (which is another fruit of the Spirit) to know that it is OK to be where you are right now. You are vulnerable when you do that, but in a good sense, because you are being genuine and true. If you let go of one path, it leaves space for another. You may not know how it will end, but you know you are headed in the right direction.

Things will turn out right; wee miracles will happen in your life that you never dreamt of.

Look deep within and what you find is Divine Love.

The greatest love you can experience is in communion with God. As you meditate this love will grow. You are connected to an infinite source of divine love and light and wisdom. Ask for what you need and let yourself receive.

I know God has a plan. I pray for the direction to follow it, patience to wait on it, knowledge to know when it comes. Within each of us, there is a silence, a silence as vast as the universe and when we experience that silence, we remember who we are

—Gunilla Norris

Your Spiritual Core

Trust in God with all your heart; seek truth and understanding. He alone knows your soul, your essence, even more deeply than you know it yourself. You do not choose your purpose; it is there already for you to discover and accept it. God already knows the way you need to go, but how you walk it is up to you.

It is essential to develop a strong core so you can stand, no matter what storm may enter your world. Your relationship with your higher self will provide you with this strength, hope, and help no matter what your challenge is.

Realise that God invites you to co-create your life. Listen to what he may be calling you to do.

Core strength is the key to living a fruitful, balanced, deep, and fulfilling life. A strong core will provide you with many benefits: personal inner power, protection, direction, and guidance in making decisions every day. I still sometimes worry about needless things, but I'm spending less time on each; I'm copping on quicker. When I find myself going into that place of worrying or stressing, getting annoyed about something, I can turn it around and say, 'OK, park it!'

When I find myself worrying about money, I may give myself five minutes to think about it, and then I'll say, 'OK, I'm handing that over now. It will be taken care of.' I know the universe has my back. I am being supported, even though I don't know how. If you believe it will all work, it will, but you need to trust, and you must not try to control how you think it *should* work.

Throughout your day, you have a choice of what you think about or focus on. If you want to think about your anxiety, you can do that for half an hour. If you don't pay attention, it may lead on to an hour or two hours, and you are no better for it. That can steal your joy.

You have a choice. You can discipline yourself to think about it for five or ten minutes and then park it. Realise that you can't do anything about it, and park it.

Do you think that you can stop bad things happening by worrying about them? Then take that five or ten minutes to think of all the things that can go wrong, as quickly as you can. If you hit on something that you can reasonably change, make a note of it; otherwise, move on to think of another worry. Most likely you will have run out of things to worry about before the time is up. Decide what to do about the worries you have noted, and then let them go.

After the event has passed, remind yourself: Did it go wrong in any of the many ways you worried about? If it did, was it as bad as you expected? Would it have been any better if you had worried more?

Either way, you need the self-discipline to say, 'I've had enough of that now. That's not who I am. That's not who I want to be.' Hand it over to God to sort out, and then you can come back to the joy of life, because that is who you were really meant to be. A lot of people worry about things they can't name clearly. For example, a lot of parents worry about their children going out at night. But the more you worry, the more you will find to worry about, until you end up worrying about the very fact that you are worrying.

Sometimes people can press a button in you, and you'll think, 'OK, there is something there that I don't like, but I'm not sure what.' Don't waste your time trying to work out the whys and wherefores of the feeling then and there.

Simply take a note of it. If it becomes unbearable, or it becomes part of a pattern and you can't work it out, then you need help or support to sort it out. It's there to challenge you, to help you to grow.

Looking Ahead

The more understanding I get and the deeper I go, the more I find life fascinating. That's where the joy is—when you look back and say, 'I never thought it would have worked out that way!'

Perhaps it's because I have known the other side of the coin, the depression and the deep dark hole. When you've come through those experiences, you look back at all the baggage you have carried. You let go of it, more comes up, and you let go of that too. Don't get me wrong; there are more challenges to come. There are bigger and harder challenges, but I am fit for them now.

The key is to use whatever you have learned whenever the challenges come up. Then you start to have a deeper faith and a deeper understanding of life and who you are.

If you adhere to the practice in this book—your self-awareness, your self-reflection, and your self-care—then improvement will come. Don't expect it to happen at a constant and steady rate.

Sometimes there may be a disruption in your routine. For example, perhaps you are away from home for a few days, and your eating isn't as good as you would like it to be. You need to be aware of what you are choosing to put into your body and how you might bring your health back into alignment. You do have to be prepared so that you do not fall into the habit of eating the first thing that comes to hand. You still have a choice, but you need to work more to exercise it. Remember to love yourself first, because if you don't fuel your body properly, you are not going to be any good to others.

> *Establishing, then committing to, and maintaining a daily spiritual practice is crucial, surrendering your life into God's hand.*
>
> —Iyanla Vanzant

The key word is discipline, which we will look at more in the next chapter. It is perhaps the hardest of the fruits of the Spirit: self-control.

CHAPTER 7

Spiritual Disciplines

Spiritual disciplines are the habits, practices, and experiences that are designed to develop, grow, and strengthen certain qualities of spirit. They are the things you do on a day-to-day basis. These disciplines train the soul. When you adhere to spiritual disciplines, you gain ability to receive insight, make better decisions, remain grounded, and become unaffected by external events. You feel inner peace, forge good habits, and can follow your own course.

If you want your spirit to be able to soar to adventurous heights, if you want to possess power, or if you want to be free, then you need discipline, and for that you need daily practice. If you adhere to it, it will keep you balanced.

Establishing Good Habits

Only you can decide what your discipline needs to be, so be gentle with yourself. Don't try to start several new habits all at once; it's better to get one firmly established before you introduce another. It's all about forming good habits that work for you. If you go off track, you need to examine why. What are you resisting? What excuses are you making, and how can you minimise them?

Choose something simple and easy to start with, something that you know you enjoy doing, or at least something that you know will make you feel better when you have done it. The following steps to forming a good habit are not very different from those that form a bad one. Perhaps you recognise them.

Have a Reason Why You Should Do It

Do you have some long-term goal that this habit will help you to accomplish? With a bad habit, you may not always be conscious what the reason is; it usually involves blaming yourself or someone else.

Remove Obstacles and Excuses

Each time you perform the habit, you reinforce it, so make it as easy as possible to start each time. You don't have to make a great effort of will. All you need do is to get into a place where you think, 'Ah, I might as well …'

Have a Trigger

Perhaps you want to do it at the same time each day, when you find yourself in a certain situation or mood, or directly before or after you do something else. With bad habits, this happens unconsciously, and it can take a lot of self-reflection to recognise the triggers. With good habits, you set the trigger deliberately, and you can ask other people to remind you, 'This is when I …'

Reduce Your Expectations

It's always easy to over-perform on bad habits. You tell yourself you'll only have one biscuit ('Ah, I might as well …'), and you end up eating the whole packet. It is likewise with good habits. Set a minimum that will give you some sense of accomplishment, and regard any extra you do as a bonus.

An Example

Perhaps you want to walk for half an hour every day. Why do you want to do that? Is it for your health, to give you time to think, or to get in touch with the land around you? Whatever the reason, be clear about it, and you will find unexpected ways to enhance your walks so that each one will be different. Remove obstacles by having a place for everything you will need on a walk, and make sure it is back there as soon as possible after you return.

Perhaps you want to establish a trigger for walking first thing in the morning. If you know that everything is set and ready the night before, then all you need do is to roll out of bed, get dressed, and go. Make sure there are no distractions for that half hour each day.

What happens if you wake one morning, and the weather is too bad for walking? When you are forming a habit, it is important to always respond to your trigger in the same way. Get up and get dressed for walking anyway. Perhaps it will clear enough for you to walk five minutes. If not, then you have the unexpected gift of a half an hour free that morning. Perhaps it has been given for a reason. Go do something else that you have been putting off.

You can't always stick to a routine because there are different things going on. I plan my meals as much as I can, and I know I need to discipline myself to do that to keep my energy levels high. We live quite a bit away from the shops, so we don't always have all the variety of produce we would like available. Sometimes we have groups on the farm, which means a lot of preparation and a lot of sandwiches, so even though it's all based round healthy eating, I end up eating a lot of bread.

When that happens, I accept it, but I may decide to take a week not eating any bread until I feel that I am back in balance. It's a choice that you make. Fasting helps you realise that you can make a choice, whether it's fasting for all food or from one particular thing, like bread or sugar. It breaks the cycle of eating something that you know is not doing you good, simply because it's there. Be creative about what you eat instead, making it something that you enjoy, as well as something that is good for you. Have some fruit for your tea, or a nice bowl of soup. What you put into your body is what you get out of it.

Taking Time in Solitude

I know I need to do this. If I don't, my mind gets too bumbled up and frazzled. It gives me a chance to step back from the business of everyday life.

Remembering Who I am

I discipline myself to do thirty minutes writing every day, at some part of the day. Sometimes I'll wake early and have the urge to write; there is something in my head that wants to get out. Creative writing is a way to getting your feelings out on paper so you can see what they are. It frees the mind to look at whatever challenge you are up against and find possible solutions.

I also make a to-do list. If you go into the quiet, take you pen, breathe and relax, and clear your head and meditate to a certain extent, then when the things that you need to do come to mind, you can write them down and set them aside for the present until you are finished.

I use meditation daily as well, whether listening to a podcast that's relevant to where I am at or simply sitting in silence. I might be faced with a challenge and not know how to handle it. In that case, I would do a meditation on surrender, hand it over to God, and ask for his help to deal with it. When you feel a new impulse, an uplifting thought, or an insight that you have never acted upon before, you should embrace the unknown, step out of your comfort zone, and cherish it like a newborn baby. God lives in the unknown, and when you allow yourself to fully embrace it, you will be free.

Another spiritual practice that I know I need is walking in and connecting with nature. Even though I do that with social farming participants, I know that I also need to take time by myself for it. Time alone is important; it's another form of self-care. I also go to a regular yoga class. It's important to know that you have that time set apart no matter what—time to move your body so you do not become stuck. When you let go of stuff, there is always something that will creep back in to challenge you again. Time alone is a good opportunity to self-reflect and become aware of those challenges.

I also like to read every day. It's like feeding your soul. I like to read poems and quotations to keep me on the path. Taking the time in peace and quiet helps you stay in touch with your higher self, or spirit, or God—whatever term you care to use. You can prompt that with questions: What do I need today? What do I need to do? Wait patiently and peacefully for the answer, and it will come. That's where the to-do list comes in: once I ask that question, my hand will take off, and I'll write.

At night, I reflect on the good things that have happened during the day and give thanks for them. When things go to plan, I give thanks for that. I used to write down maybe ten things that I was grateful for, but now I find that they come to mind automatically. Wherever I am at right now, I keep saying to myself that I know the universe has my back and that it's behind me, working through me for the good of whatever is next. All these practices take me forward and help me evolve and grow.

The Big Thing

The big thing that I have learned throughout my time is that if you focus on yourself, everything else usually takes care of itself. It's not that you are the only person that matters. It's not even being selfish. If you focus on changing yourself, everything else around you will eventually shift and change too, because you are seeing things differently. You have a different perception, so you react differently.

Other people start to reflect that change in you. It's simply being aware so that that you don't get caught up or sucked into other people's dramas.

Sometimes people focus on others to avoid focusing on themselves. I know I have done this in the past. A lot of people, because of their pain or because of where they are at, do not want to look at themselves, so it suits them to focus on other people—if only they did things the right way, then everything would be all right. When you do that, you get into the blame game, blaming others for your shortcomings.

The big thing is taking ownership and taking responsibility for your actions. Sometimes people go into jobs and stay in them simply because they are paid good money, but they are not happy. If they listened to themselves, they might realise that they should be doing something else.

You don't have to give up your job, but you can certainly work towards what you feel that you could be doing or should be doing. That's more authentic. It's more real, and it takes less energy in life to do what you love doing. Otherwise you get stuck in victim mode: 'Poor me! Look at all I do for you, and you never do anything for me!'

Chapter 8

What Is Love?

We're not really taught that God loves us, are we? People say it, but it comes across as a great big book that holds a record of all you have done wrong.

In our educational system, there is so much to learn—and there is so much to unlearn as well. It's a matter of peeling back all that you have learned, deciding whether it is true and helpful, and creating your life for yourself with a clean book. You need to peel away the untruths and lies that you have been told. You don't realise the impact of every experience that you've had as you came along your life until you take the time to look back at it.

If you go back and put love at the centre of it, you may find it creates a better meaning for everything. We all have the story of our lives, but whenever you peel all that back, you realize who you are at your core. When we get married, sometimes we are taught that is the fulfilment of your life. But there is so much more. What is love for you? What does it represent? What have you learned that you can relate to your own life? Where is your awareness and knowledge of your own love? I have learned that you need to love yourself first before you can love others. You need to feed your own life before you can feed another's. You need the groundedness of a sense of self, of who you are. Working with others doesn't let you off the hook regarding working on yourself. Unless you use self-reflection, you lose track of who you are and where you are going.

Beliefs

As you develop your awareness, you get to a place where you start to question your beliefs. You think to yourself, 'Where did I get that from?' Then you ask yourself, 'Does that really serve me right now?'

Sometimes, that may mean re-examining something that you once believed and seeing it in a different way. For example, I took myself out of the church, but now I am back, and I look at God in a different way. Thirty years ago, I would have been heavily involved in the church, but I would have been lost. I had no understanding or awareness of it at all. I was there, but I was simply going through the motions because it was part of the norm. You do these things to fit in and be part of the community. It's what my neighbour does, and this neighbour, and that neighbour. You go with the flow.

If you take yourself out of it, you look at everybody else, and you'll think you are alone. You seem different, the odd one out. That can be a lonely place to be, but your awareness takes you into a different perspective. Your life becomes richer as you find other people to relate to who are on their own journeys and have similar thoughts and feelings.

If you take yourself on a journey of self-discovery, it is important not to isolate yourself or find another bubble to hide inside. Don't do it alone; search out there, because there are other people on your wavelength. That is a big part of the self-discovery process. You know in your heart that you don't want to follow the norm of what everybody else is doing. You want to find your own way, but you need to look to others who are also maybe finding their way, and you should connect because you can draw support from each other.

That is important no matter who you are or what journey you are on. Too many people think they must suffer in silence because there is no one to whom they can talk. I have been there and done that. You can eat, sleep, do your work, and believe that you are alone, and that knock years off your life if you let it. I suffered in silence for ages until I realised that I wasn't the only one. We all need each other. We need people who are hurting and searching, not just people who have it all together already.

You can learn so much from others, and others can learn so much from you. I've found this in social farming. I work with people who have mental health problems or disabilities. They all have a gift to share.

Religion and Self-Help

You are brought up in one denomination, and you are living in a community with other denominations. In fact, when you peel it all back, you realise that we are all one, and we are all seeking the same thing. The things that humans have instituted with regards to religion can separate us if we let them. That's where the ego comes in. A church or other organisation has an ego of its own and its own agenda. When I worked in an organisation for victims of the Troubles, I felt the agenda there. I was out in the community and working with people who had post-traumatic stress disorder. Other people sometimes have an agenda to keep them in victim mode because, as they see it, there are 'our victims' and 'their victims', and 'our victims' have suffered more.

The aim of any self-help group should be to empower people. If there is a conflict of values, it can cause a tension that you need to work through until you see where it is coming from.

Even in our education system, teachers are put under a tremendous amount of pressure to get so many kids through transfer tests. Sometimes kids can get lost in that. That is a result of the belief that you need to have a grade A to be of any importance. Sometimes people get caught up in cheating as a result. If they get away with it once, they create another experience, and another one and another one.

They feel compelled to keep on that path whether they want to or not. I think there is too much emphasis on having to achieve measurable targets, and there could be more placed on children's creativity. I would not even have thought about writing a book if I had not come full circle.

Sense of Self

You need to have a good sense of self. Again, it depends on your conditioning and your belief system. There are good things in your upbringing, and you need to find those and hold on to them. For example, there was a time after we got married when we did farming. Then we went into education, insurance, and other things. It took us away from the groundedness of the farm. We were attached to the land. When you go away from that, you sort of lose yourself. Then when you come back to the land again, you need to connect. That's why we went into social farming: it's finding that connection again and moving it in a different direction. It's using your roots in a good way, for the development of other people.

I have a passion, and it had been sleeping for years, but it always came back. It was the sense that if I helped myself, then I could help others. That gets me excited to get up in the morning.

What do you want to do or create in your life? What's your passion? What have you always wanted to do that fear or something else has held you back from doing? When life takes you on a different journey, you will come back to that. How can you use your learning and your journey to connect with others and take them with you?

Your story, your journey, is unique. No one else can do what you were meant to do.

CHAPTER 9

Creating a Life That You Love

A life that you love begins with respect, and respect begins with yourself. As you pull back from being used and abused by others, eventually you get to a place of being able to say no.

Respecting your body is an essential aspect of self-respect. Respect it by eating healthy food, exercising, and lowering stress. Respect yourself enough to walk away from anything that no longer serves you or makes you happy. Respecting yourself can be difficult at times. Not everything is within your control, and you cannot control how others act. However, you can control how you treat yourself. Don't settle for anything less than you deserve. We all deserve the very best in life. Forgive yourself for any mistakes that you have made. The more you believe in yourself, the easier it will be to treat yourself with love and respect. Making yourself feel good physically is one of the ultimate ways of respecting yourself. Treat your body as you would the body of someone you love. Don't compare yourself to others; comparison is the thief of joy. Simply remind yourself that no matter how well you know people, you don't know everything about their lives.

No one can make you feel badly about yourself without your permission.

Freedom

Now you feel that you are free and have let go a lot from your past. Now you have a choice in creating your future. So why not create one that you love? You create your life through your thoughts: what you focus on most is what will appear in your life.

Creating a life that you love is very much to an individual's taste. It's up to you—your choices and your creation. I understand that there are still some things we can't change, and we all have responsibilities, but I still think you can choose how to deal with them.

For me, creating an authentic life starts with looking within. This is an ongoing process, using the tools I discussed earlier. I use meditation daily as part of my spiritual practice. Discipline is crucial in this. Sit quietly and breathe, connecting with yourself and your inner truth.

There are many ways of learning, and for me, one of the best is experimental learning. Try it for yourself and see how you can get your message across. Try the simplest thing that can possibly work. Notice how it succeeds and how it fails, and use that knowledge to try again.

Use whatever you have on hand. Creating a life that you love is about aligning yourself with your core values. For me, it's journaling and gardening, growing vegetables and flowers, cooking wholesome meals using produce that is taken from the farm or purchased organically, baking or moving my body through exercise, walking in nature, and yoga. I avoid stimulants such as coffee, sugar, fizzy drinks, alcohol, GMO food, white bread, unhealthy oils, margarine, and processed foods.

Follow your own compass. Live life outside the box because that is where the magic happens. Nurture relationships with family and friends. Choose to immerse yourself with like-minded people and speak your truth; this leads to deep conversations that become more meaningful, as well as opportunities to create and expand on new life experiences. See beauty, love, and value in ordinary things. Take care of your body. Practice gratitude.

Use whatever you love doing and incorporate it into the message that you want to get across. That's where self-awareness and self-reflection come in. For example, if you are doing a workshop, take time after it is over to reflect on how it has gone. Then ask yourself how you can improve on that for the next time round.

If you were to sit in a room for a week with the blinds closed, how would you feel? You would have low motivation and low enthusiasm to get up and do anything. For people in a depressed state of mind, that's what their picture of the world looks like.

I can only go from my own experiences. As you shed the layers of your onion, working on why you've been depressed your life becomes brighter, and then you crave more of it. You learn new patterns of thinking, you learn new patterns of being positive, and the old pattern goes away along with the negative stuff. I call this raising your vibration—moving yourself up a level and making yourself more open.

If you stay in that negative state, the law of attraction comes in, and you attract more negative stuff into your life. But if you are bright and cheerful, and are looking out, what you focus on is what you get. If you are looking out, you can see what's coming. I am in a place now where I don't want any more of that negativity. I've been there. I have experienced all of that and let go of all of that. This is where I'm at, and this is where I want to be, because we weren't put on this earth to stay stuck. We were put on this earth to be in a more joyful state.

Life is good, and life can be better. Through your own choices, you can create a life that is positive. Pay attention to what is in your thought processes and catch yourself if you are heading back down the wrong path. What is going on in the lives of the people around you is their choice. If you want to be there, you'll be there, but they're not taking you there with them. You can always do something else.' If you can share that, if you can get them to think, 'OK, maybe I do have a choice of how I handle this,' it can improve their day.

You can only work on the things where you feel you have a choice. If you work on those, perhaps you can come to see other places where you have a choice.

Certainly, there are some things you can't change, and that's OK. Sometimes when I can't change something, I'll hand that over to my higher self and say, 'Can you change that, or can you show me a way to change it? Or if I need to do something, can you please let me know?'

It's OK if no answer comes, because it may be that it's not ready to be changed, or maybe there's some other work to be done. Maybe you're not ready, and you need to be looking in other areas. You need to go with the flow of life because what you resist will persist. Life's not meant to be a struggle. It should be joyful.

That doesn't mean that you should deny what's there. Some people try to cope by denying that they have problems. You do have a choice. If you dwell on that place of thinking about something in a negative way, you'll attract more and more negativity.

Connecting with Helpers

Recently, I have noticed something that I am paying more attention to. At certain times throughout the day—it comes every now and again—I get a ringing in my ears.

It's telling me to listen. Whenever I hear it, I will take myself to a quiet place, breathe, and sit for five minutes until I get messages. Then I go to the book and write them down. When I get this ringing in the ears, it's telling me to slow down because there is something I should be listening to.

It's hard to explain, but it's there, and it's important for me to spend the time listening for the message whenever it happens. My hand will take off, and I'll start to write. I could have a page, two pages, or three pages. It will tell me what I need to do and how I need to discipline myself, or if there's something going on around me, and I need to recognise it and to pull back.

It comes back to that sense of self-awareness again, to that calm centre point. Pay attention to what's going on, take a moment and breathe and tune in, and believe that the messages are coming through to get you in a different place.

While using the breath in meditation, you may visualise a white light flowing into your body, cleansing every cell.

Say to yourself, 'Be still, be still,' and a sense of calm will result. Another example of a visualisation you can use is to imagine that you are in the shower; visualise the water washing away all the stresses of the day.

If you have a question, you may invite guides to advise you on how to move forward. I keep a journal nearby to record any information given in this way. I simply write down and question and wait and listen for the answers. This is channelling from the world of Spirit. I do this daily as part of my practice.

When I talk of connecting with Spirit, I do not mean individual spirits in some spirit otherworld but rather your higher self—that part of you that already knows where your problem lies and what you should do about it. Use whatever visualisations are useful to you. If you believe in angels or in nature spirits, then do not be surprised if that is what you see.

Remember, it is the message that is important, not the messenger. Is it helpful? If not, let it go. You also can ask your guides to clear any negative energy that's around you and replace it with powerful healing energy and love, including trimming back any relationships that drain you.

The more negative energy you collect, the harder it will be for your spirit guides to connect. Messages can come in many forms. Sometimes you don't know at the time what the message is, but you know you have received something because of the awe and beauty in what has just happened. You feel that emotion because it connects with what is happening in your life at that specific time. You have seen a symbol that highlights something to which you should pay attention, and eventually that connection will become clear to you.

You may perhaps look it up later in a book of symbols and find a meaning there that resonates. For example, one day while on a walk, I saw two ducks taking off in flight, and I had that sudden felling of awe. I looked it up and found it was a symbol of joyfulness, naturally taking off. The more you learn and understand such meanings, the more you will notice them. I believe that these are messages or hints or nudges for my learning in life. Watching out for them makes you more observant, using your five senses more, and they give you clarity around things so that you know who you are and where you are in the world.

At home, I have five geese and four ducks. I had ten total, but one of them died. There were eleven of us in the family. My brother Albert was shot as a result of the Troubles, and then my brother Robbie died. I led the nine fowl out to the field every day. Everything is like that: it fits if you want it to fit. It is a sign if you can see it.

I build that into my daily practice of self-awareness because otherwise, you can go round and round on your hamster wheel and never get off it. I use it as a means of grounding myself. I calm my breath and then ask questions. What is it that I need to do today? How can I move ahead with what I want to do? How can I improve a certain aspect of my life? When I have social farming participants, what activities can I use to help them along?

If you breathe into yourself, listen, and ask the question, you normally get an answer. It's simply a matter of taking the time in peace and quiet.

It's not just answers to the big questions. Sometimes

there is something small that has been niggling you, and you hadn't noticed.

Spring Seeds

Spring is about renewal. Spring is about planting seeds of hope. I'm thinking about spring, and I'm planning the seeds of what can be. Once you get to autumn, then you are reaping what you showed in the springtime. Winter is a time to rest; we aren't supposed to be sowing seeds then. I don't know what is coming, but I feel the vibration is rising. It will sort itself.

> *Whatever you sow, you reap. Your thoughts are seeds, and the harvest you reap depends on the seeds that you plant.*
>
> —Rhonda Byrne

I have found that my purpose is to help people find inner peace and happiness. Your purpose may be different, but you will find it and create a life that you love around it.

What resonates with me is using my intuition—a deep sense of knowing when things are right.

Investment in you for others

Going for help and healing is an investment in you. As you take back your power, consider how you can use it for the betterment of yourself and other individuals. Don't try to pay for it with work that contradicts what you are learning. What you do at work should resonate with what you have learned. It should reinforce it for you and for others, helping them as well, so you are actually enjoying the work that you are doing. You are being authentic, and you are speaking your truth.

I've been asking myself how I can use those aspects with this book when it is finished. What are the opportunities, and where can I take it? Opportunities will easily come. I will see an opportunity that reflects something I have put in the book, and I will take it. It comes naturally. It comes from the heart, and there is no fear behind it.

If you come across as genuine and ready to share some part of your story, that will resonate with the people to whom you are talking. Perhaps they will learn from it.

Create your life with the result of what you have learned from your spiritual journey. Have respect for yourself for all that you have come through and let go of. Value the wisdom you have gained from that and consider how you can use that to have an income that reflects that.

I've found that the more I work on myself, the more I can bring other people alongside me, and the more it gives me a freedom so I can step back and let somebody else take control. You give others a chance to build themselves up. You do it in a quiet way, letting them express themselves, heal, or do whatever they need to do.

Mabel Campbell

Social Farming and its benefits

This journey has brought me to get involved in social farming which began through an EU-funded Interreg project back in 2013. The Leitrim Development Company was one partner; the University of Ulster and University College Dublin were others. The Department of Agriculture and Rural Affairs and the Health Trust were also involved. They wanted ten farms in the North and ten farms in the South to take part as a pilot study, and it was very oversubscribed, but our farm was chosen.

Social farming is using the resources of the land, animals, and growing of vegetables and flowers for the health and well-being of others. One day a week for a period of thirty weeks, three participants or service users would come to the farm and join in the farming activities. These were people recovering from mental health problems, referred through the Community Mental Health team, and the universities did research on their progression. The results can be downloaded from the social farming website here.

www.socialfarmingacrossborders.org

It was all about giving people who were isolated within the community a structure and purpose for their week. If they came to the farm on a certain day, they knew they had to get up, get ready, and be prepared to go on the bus. We encouraged them to engage in activities on the farm by supporting and working alongside them.

They joined us at the table during mealtimes, and they didn't do much talking at the beginning. It took time, and we had to start with very small things. For example, if I was feeding sheep with buckets of feed nuts, I would show and explain what I was doing, and then I'd let them fill the buckets from the meal bin. I showed them how it could be done, and then I let them do for themselves and take part in the activity. It was the same with planting seeds for example in springtime. I would provide the necessary materials to complete the task, and I guided and encouraged them.

As they stuck with it, I found them starting to talk, open up, and share, and they took ownership of the tasks.

They developed relationships between each other as their confidence grew. When you have people who are quite vulnerable and tender, they really need the time and patience to bring them to a place where they can be more confident.

Social farming is about normalising everyday life, dropping the labels at the farm gate. They are taking part in ordinary, everyday activities that are meaningful. You're not setting up something that is created solely for people's health and well-being; you are letting them become a part of something that has a meaning of its own. The care for the individual person is mirrored in the care for the animals and the land. If you teach someone to nurture a seed to grow, people can learn to care and nurture their own selves.

You need to slow down, you can't rush things, and that requires patience. Social farming suits smallholdings; That's the beauty about it: it can contribute to society by meeting the needs of others. I got involved because I wanted to make a difference in the lives of the individuals that I worked with. I knew the therapeutic benefits of working with plants and animals and this sat very much with my values as a person.

From that first pilot project, we set up a community interest company. We have continued to provide the service delivery of social farming and my learning from it has helped me shape the contents of this book.

The Future

Working with people requires me to work on myself. As I continue to grow and evolve on my personal journey, I have to give thanks to all the experiences and challenges that I have encountered along the way. I have no doubt as I go forward from here that more opportunities will open up for me and I am excited to what that may bring. The knowledge I share will guide me into new situations and experiences in which I can only thrive.

"For you I hope I have planted a seed, both literally and metaphorically. With a little understanding, together we can help our lives grow into something magnificent."

Charts and Diagrams

The Chakras

The Root Chakra	At the base of your spine, the tailbone.
Physical Imbalances	Problems with legs, feet rectum, immune system, male reproductive parts, prostate, arthritis, knee pain, sciatica, eating disorders, constipation.
Emotional Imbalances	Anxiety about basic survival needs: money, shelter, and food. Inability to provide necessities.
The Feeling of Balance	Supported, grounded. A sense of safety and connection to the physical world.
The Lesson	Self-preservation.

The Sacral Chakra	Two inches below your navel.
Physical Imbalances	Sexual and reproductive issues, urinary problems, kidney dysfunctions. Hip, pelvic, and lower back pain.
Emotional Imbalances	Problems with relationships. Inability to express emotions. Fears of impotence, betrayal, addictions.
The Feeling of Balance	Ability to take risks. Creative, committed, passionate, sexual, and outgoing.
The Lesson	Honour others.
The Solar Plexus Chakra	Three inches above your navel.
Physical Imbalances	Digestive problems, liver dysfunction, chronic fatigue, high blood pressure, diabetes, stomach ulcers, pancreas, gall bladder, and colon.
Emotional Imbalances	Issues of personal power and self-esteem. The inner critic. Fear of rejection, criticism, and physical appearance.
The Feeling of Balance	Self-respect and self-compassion. In control, assertive, confident.
The Lesson	Self-acceptance.

The Heart Chakra	Upper chest.
Physical Imbalances	Asthma, heart disease, lung issues, and breast issues. Lymphatic system, upper back, and shoulder problems. Arm and wrist pain.
Emotional Imbalances	Issues of the heart; over-loving, jealousy, abandonment, anger, bitterness. Fear of loneliness.
The Feeling of Balance	Joy, gratitude, love, compassion. Forgiving and trusted.
The Lesson	I love.

The Throat Chakra	Neck.
Physical Imbalances	Thyroid, sore throat, laryngitis, jaw pain, ear infections, ulcers, facial problems, neck and shoulder pain.
Emotional Imbalances	Issues of self-expression in communication, spoken or written. Fear of no choice or power. Lack of willpower or self-control.
The Feeling of Balance	Free flow of words, expression, and communication. Honest and truthful yet firm. Good listener.
The Lesson	Speak up and let your voice be heard.

The Third Eye Chakra	Centre of the forehead.
Physical Imbalances	Headaches, blurred vision, sinus issues, eyestrain, seizures, hearing loss, hormone function.
Emotional Imbalances	Moodiness, volatility. Inability to look at your own fears and learn from others. Daydreaming and fantasy.
The Feeling of Balance	Clear, focused. Can determine between truth and illusion. Open to receiving wisdom and insight.
The Lesson	See the big picture.
The Crown Chakra	Top of the head.
Physical Imbalances	Depression; inability to learn; sensitivity to light, sound, or environment.
Emotional Imbalances	Issues with self-knowledge and greater power. Rigid thoughts on religion and spirituality. Constant confusion. Prejudice and over-analysis. Fear of alienation.
The Feeling of Balance	Living in the present moment, with an unshakeable trust in your inner guidance.
The Lesson	Live mindfully.

The Wheel of Life

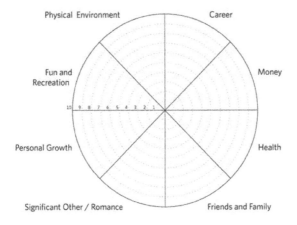

The wheel of life is a tool used in life coaching to assess in which area of your life you want to make improvements. Mark a point in each segment to indicate where you feel you are. A distance from the centre of zero would indicate complete dissatisfaction, and ten indicates complete satisfaction. Join the points together to make a graph; then consider which points you want to move outwards and what you need to do to move them.

A Sample Self-Care Plan

Physical	*Walk three to four times a week *Go to the gym two times a week *Go to yoga once a week *Drink water *Make home-cooked meals instead of fast food *Declutter one room at a time
Mental and Emotional	*Learn to say no when I need to *Talk with a trusted friend or healer *Journal my feelings *Keep a gratitude journal *Visit somewhere different once a month
Social	*Meet up with friends once a week *Plan family outings/get-togethers *Get involved in a group of interest
Spiritual	*Meditate *Journal *Read books on spirituality or healing *Spend time in nature *Have an energy healing and clearing

Lightning Source UK Ltd.
Milton Keynes UK
UKHW012248101120
373159UK00001B/49